OXFORD BOOKWORMS LIBRARY

Factfiles

Global Issues

ALEX RAYNHAM

AND RACHEL BLADON

Stage 3 (1000 headwords)

Series Editor: Rachel Bladon

Founder Factfiles Editor: Christine Lindop

OXFORD
UNIVERSITY PRESS

Great Clarendon Street, Oxford, OX2 6DP, United Kingdom

Oxford University Press is a department of the University of Oxford.
It furthers the University's objective of excellence in research, scholarship,
and education by publishing worldwide. Oxford is a registered trade
mark of Oxford University Press in the UK and in certain other countries

ISBN: 978 0 19 462458 9

A complete recording of this Bookworms edition
of *Global Issues* is available.

Printed in China

Word count (main text): 9,227

For more information on the Oxford Bookworms Library,
visit www.oup.com/elt/gradedreaders

ACKNOWLEDGEMENTS

Cover image: House facades, Mumbai. Frank Bienewald/Lightrocket via Getty Images.

The publisher would like to thank the following for permission to reproduce photographs:
123RF pp.2 (map/Micelinjo, cotton field/Noam Amonn, spinning cotton yarn/
Yang Yu); Alamy Images pp.2 (garment factory/Liba Taylor), 6 (R. M. Nunes),
8 (imageBROKER), 11 (Mark Phillips), 13 (scientist/Image Source Plus), 18 (crop
sprayer/imageBROKER), 29 (seed store exterior/Tim E White), 31 (mosquito
net/Prisma by Dukas Presseagentur GmbH), 38 (Purepix), 39 (Pacific Press),
55 (bananas/Justin Kase zsixz), 52 (Mark Thomas), 57 (Zoonar GmbH); Sanjukta
Basu p.53; Luke Casey p.51; Fairtrade p.55 (logo); Getty Images pp.2 (Internet
company/Bloomberg), 5 (Kohei Hara), 10 (Dinodia Photo), 14 (Jonas Gratzer/
LightRocket), 20 (Paul Sutherland Photography/Photographer's Choice),
21 (Bloomberg), 22 (Natalie Fobes/Science Faction), 27 (Martyn Aim/Corbis News),
29 (seed packets/AFP Stringer), 33 (Issouf Sanogo/AFP), 34 (Stewart Cohen/Pam
Ostrow/Blend Images), 42 (Spencer Platt), 43 (NurPhoto), 45 (vlogger/Antonio
Diaz/Mexico), 49 (robot/Yoshikazu Tsuno), 54 (Michel Porro/Contour); iStock
pp.2 (boy/michaeljung), 36 (Junpinzon); Naturepl.com p.28 (Luke Massey);
Oxford University Press RF pp.25 (solar panels/Shutterstock), 30 (Shutterstock),
31 (mosquito/Shutterstock); PA Images p.49 (driverless car/Fabio De Paola/PA
Archive); Rex/Shutterstock pp.40 (Abir Abdullah/EPA), 50 (Str/EPA); Science Photo
Library p.7 (Johnny Grieg), 44 (NASA); Shutterstock pp. iv (MarcelClemens),
4 (Alex Oakenman), 12 (insects/Shanti Hesse, seaweed/MaxCab), 16 (JoeyPhoto),
17 (Daulon), 19 (air pollution/elwynn, landfill/Vchal), 23 (Vaclav Sebek), 25 (wind
turbines/Noradoa, dam/Kat72, geothermal plant/N. Minton), 26 (Pryzmat),
35 (PreechaB), 45 (teens on phones/Bokan), 46 (People), 74 (Macknimal).

The publisher would also like to thank Rick Sampedro for his help in developing this book.

CONTENTS

1 What are global issues?

Right now, astronauts are living and working 400 kilometres above us in space — and the world looks very different from up there. Astronauts can see how beautiful Earth is, and when they look at the lights of the world's great cities at night, they know that for many people, this is a wonderful time to be alive.

But astronauts can also see how our world is changing. They look down and see the dirty waters of great rivers like the Mississippi, and fires from trees burning in the Amazon and Indonesia. Over time, their photographs from space show us how the world's great forests are becoming smaller, how some of the hottest countries are becoming drier, and how every year there is more plastic in the ocean.

Astronauts can see how we are changing the environment, but there are many other problems that they cannot see from space. They cannot see how many people go to bed hungry every night and do not have clean water to drink. They cannot see the millions of children who are not able to go to school, or the animals that are dying because their homes are disappearing.

These problems, which are important for people and countries all around the world, are called 'global issues'. So, what are the biggest global issues today, and why do we need to know about them? What is happening to our world, and is it in danger?

2 A changing world

The world has begun to change very fast – and as it changes, the global issues that are important in our lives change, too.

Globalization

In Utrecht, in the Netherlands, a Dutch boy opens a package. Inside, there is a T-shirt which the boy has been waiting for. On the T-shirt, it says *Made in Bangladesh*, but the T-shirt was not only made in Bangladesh. The material for the T-shirt came from cotton plants which grew on a farm in Arkansas, USA. Later, the cotton went to Mexico. There, factory machines from Japan and Germany made it into material. The material then went by ship to Dhaka in Bangladesh, and there it was made into a T-shirt. From Dhaka, it travelled to Guangzhou in China. A Chinese company sold the T-shirt on the internet and sent it out to the Netherlands.

One hundred years ago, many companies only made and sold things in their home country. But in today's global economy, companies produce and sell things all over the world. It is becoming easier and easier to travel from one place to another, and to do business with people who live thousands of kilometres away. This is called 'globalization'. Because of globalization, when something happens in one part of the world, there are changes for countries and people everywhere. So in 2008, for example, problems with some of the banks in the USA caused an economic crash around the world.

1 Cotton plants growing on a farm

2 Making material from cotton

3 Making a T-shirt from material

4 Selling the T-shirt on the internet

Population

In 1950, the world had a population of 2.6 billion people, but today, there are more people than that just in China and India. By 2016, there were 7.5 billion people in the world – and that number was growing by about one million every five days! By 2050, there will probably be about 9.5 billion people on Earth.

The world's population is growing fastest in some of the countries that have the least money. For example, Malawi and Burundi in Africa are two of the countries where the population is growing fastest, but they are also two of the poorest countries in the world. In places like these, it is already difficult for many people to get good food, clean water, and healthcare, and to find a safe home. With bigger populations, these problems may become worse.

Some other countries have the opposite problem: their populations are getting smaller. For example, the population of the Cook Islands, in the Pacific, is falling every year. This is because people are having fewer children than before, and because many are leaving the islands to go to bigger places like New Zealand.

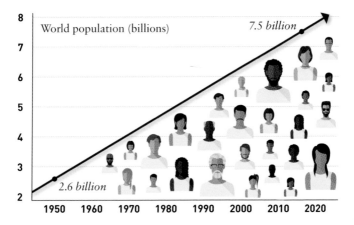

Populations also fall when countries are at war, and people leave to escape the fighting, or are killed. After a war started in Syria in 2011, millions of people left their homes there, and the population of the country became smaller and smaller.

If a country's population becomes smaller, it can be a problem. For example, shops cannot sell many things, and businesses and universities cannot find enough workers or students.

Another important change in the world's population is that today there are more and more older people. In many parts of the world, healthcare is much better now, so people are living longer. They are having fewer children, too. In Japan, more than a quarter of the population is now over sixty-five, and by 2055, people think that 40% of the Japanese population will be in their late sixties and seventies.

Japan's population is getting older.

Growing cities

As the world population grows, and more and more people move away from their homes to look for work, cities are getting bigger. In 1950, only 30% of the world's population lived in cities, and Tokyo was the only 'megacity' (a city with more than ten million people). But today, more than half of the world's population lives in cities and towns, and there are megacities all over the world, like Delhi, Beijing, Istanbul, and São Paulo. In the next one hundred years, some megacities may be home to between 50 and 100 million people!

São Paulo

Inequality

The UK is one of the richest countries in the world, and in 2015, there were nearly one million British millionaires (people who had more than one million UK pounds). But in that same year, more than half a million people in the UK used food banks – places where food is collected and given to those who do not have enough money to buy what they need. In many countries, there is this problem of inequality: the lives of the richest people are very different from the lives of the poorest. And this problem is becoming bigger all the time. In 2017, there was a report on inequality by Oxfam, a group of organizations which work with people in some of the poorest countries. The report said that eight of the richest people in the world own the same wealth as the poorest 3.6 billion.

Inequality between people in the same country is a problem, and inequality between countries is a problem, too. Most of the world's wealth is in rich countries. Life can be easier for people in rich countries because these places usually have good modern hospitals, schools, cities, and roads. But most of the world's population lives in developing countries – places that have much less wealth, like the countries of sub-Saharan Africa.

In Nigeria, sub-Saharan Africa

Think how much your family spends every day on food, drink, clothes, and your home. Nearly half of the people in our world live on less than US$2.50 a day. They do not have enough food or water, and often have to live on the streets or in slums – dirty, noisy places with bad buildings.

Slums in Haiti

3   Water and food

Although the world's population is growing very fast, there is enough food and water for everybody – but today, about 800 million people are hungry, and about one in ten people do not have clean water near to their home.

When families do not have enough money, it is difficult for them to buy good food and eat well. This is bad for everyone in the family – but it is very dangerous for children, because children need the right food to grow and be strong.

Water

The United Nations – an important organization which works to protect people's human rights – said in 2010 that every person in the world should have 50–100 litres of water a day for drinking, cooking, and washing. The United Nations also said that water should be safe and easy to get (taking less than thirty minutes to collect).

But in developing countries, millions of people die from diseases because they do not have enough good drinking water, or because there is not enough water to keep themselves and their homes clean. Nearly one billion people – most of them women – have to walk several kilometres to get water every day.

There are water problems all around the world. Water can become dirty in many different ways, for example from pollution, rubbish, floods, and bad pipes. In the city of Flint, in Michigan, USA, there were very bad problems after the city began getting its water from the Flint River in 2014.

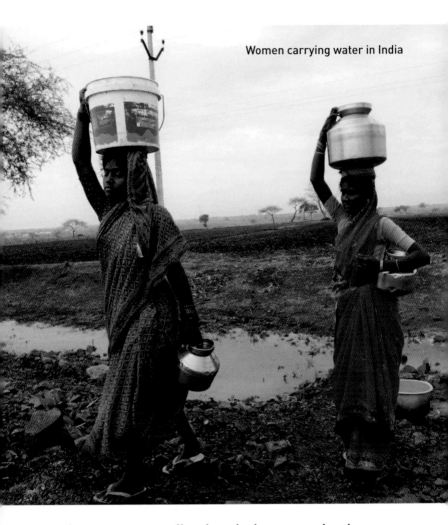

Women carrying water in India

The river is very polluted, and there were also dangerous chemicals in the water from old water pipes.

In many places, there are also problems with wasted water. Water is lost every day, in rich countries and developing countries, because pipes are old and breaking. Many countries also have less water now because people have built on wetlands – areas of land that were full of water.

Food waste

People in many parts of the world are hungry every day, but in some places, a lot of food is thrown away. Food is wasted when farmers cannot sell their crops, or when restaurants and supermarkets make or buy more food than they need – but most food waste happens at home, and the problem is biggest in rich countries.

Every year, people and businesses in the USA waste about 60 billion kilograms of food – 33% of all the food in the country. Companies use a lot of energy when they make food and move it from place to place to sell – so when food is not used, energy is wasted and pollution is produced, for nothing. Food decomposes – it breaks into smaller and smaller pieces, and goes back into the land. But when it decomposes, it produces strong gases that are very bad for the environment.

Food waste

Where our food comes from

A lot of our food comes from very far away. People in Italy can buy coffee from Brazil and fish from Spain – and in shops in Japan, there is meat from the USA and vegetables from China. But some people think that when food is moved across the world, this wastes energy and causes pollution.

Even when people eat food that was grown in their country, it has probably travelled far. Until recent times, sugar cane, the plant that produces sugar, grew on the island of Maui, in Hawaii – but the sugar from Maui travelled to San Francisco, where it was made into white sugar, and then to New York, where it was packaged, before it came back to Maui. So the sugar that people ate in Maui had grown a few kilometres away, but had travelled about 16,000 kilometres.

The future of food

Because the world's population is growing, people are now thinking about how we will be able to make or grow enough food for everyone in the future. We may need to eat other food that we can get easily, and which we can produce in a way that does not use a lot of energy, land, and money. For example, two billion people in the world already eat insects, but more people may start eating them, because they are easier to produce than farm animals. They also give us a lot of energy, and are very healthy. Sea plants may become a more popular food in the future for the same reasons.

Insects

Sea plants

Scientists are looking at new ways of making food, too. They have found a way to grow meat from animal cells – the smallest living parts of animals. Some people think that if we grow meat in this way in the future, we will not need to keep farm animals any more.

Some companies are also now making 'GM' (genetically modified) foods. GM foods are made when scientists add DNA from other species to food plants like fruits and vegetables, to change them. For example, they can make the plants bigger and stronger, and easier to grow. Some GM crops can grow well even in droughts – times when there is no rain at all – and other GM crops do not get diseases. Because of this, some people think that GM foods will be important in the future.

But many people are worried about changing food in this way. They think that growing GM crops may damage the environment, and they also think that eating GM foods may be bad for our health.

GM crops

4 The environment

The small island country of Kiribati sits among beautiful coral reefs in the Pacific Ocean. It is home to more than 100,000 people at the moment. But Kiribati's president has said that, before 2080, everyone will need to leave.

Kiribati's towns and villages are less than two metres above the sea – and every year, the sea is getting higher. The people of Kiribati know that, if the sea does not stop rising, they will soon need to leave their homes forever.

Kiribati is not the only place in the world where people will have to change their lives in the future. There will be changes for many of us, because of one of the biggest global issues today: problems with the environment.

Flooding in Kiribati

Global warming

Scientists say that world temperatures are about 1°C warmer today than 250 years ago – and by 2050, the temperature may be another 2°C warmer. We call this 'global warming'. 2°C does not sound like a lot, but for the world around us, it is very serious.

The oceans cover 71% of Earth, and when temperatures go up, the oceans rise, because water expands – gets bigger – when it gets warmer. The oceans will rise even more because the ice that covers the Arctic and Antarctic is beginning to melt into the sea as temperatures rise. Antarctica is losing about 100 square kilometres of ice every year.

Some people think that if global warming continues, by the year 2100, the world's seas may be two metres higher than they are today. If that happens, great megacities like Mumbai, New York, and Shanghai, which are not high above the sea, may be in danger.

Climate change

Scientists say that our climate (the temperature, and how much rain, snow, sun, and wind we have) is becoming different from how it once was. This is called 'climate change'.

Many people are very worried about climate change, and think that it is already making the world's weather much wilder than before. Because of climate change, they say, strong winds are destroying houses, dry forests are burning, and heavy rain is damaging farmers' crops and flooding the land. It is becoming difficult for farmers to grow food in some places.

If the climate continues to change, it will make life harder for many people. Some places will have more snow, some will have more heavy rain, and others will have longer droughts.

There will be more storms, too, and many people may have to leave the land where they live and work. Scientists also think that some plant and animal species will become extinct – none of them will be able to stay alive any more.

Drought in Thailand

The greenhouse effect

So, if our climate is changing, what are the causes? To understand this, we need to know about the 'greenhouse effect'. The greenhouse effect is important for our world because it keeps Earth warm enough for us to live here. But how does the greenhouse effect work?

When energy from the light of the sun hits Earth, most of it goes back out into space. But around Earth, there are 'greenhouse gases' (like carbon dioxide and methane) which make a kind of 'cover' in the air. They catch some of the sun's energy and make Earth warmer. We call this 'the greenhouse effect' because these gases help to keep Earth warm, just like a glass greenhouse keeps plants warm.

Greenhouse gases have always been in the air above us. They are made by animals and other living things. But since the eighteenth and nineteenth centuries, when many countries began to industrialize – build machines and factories – we have been producing more and more carbon dioxide. In some countries, people burn forests to get more land for farming or for houses, and this produces more carbon dioxide, too.

Scientists think that, with all this extra carbon dioxide, Earth's greenhouse gases have become thicker. Because of this, less of the sun's energy can escape back into space. So Earth is getting warmer, scientists say – and the rise in the world's temperature is causing climate change.

The greenhouse effect

Greenhouse gases

Pollution

Scientists say that climate change is not the only problem of living in an industrialized world. Every day, dangerous and dirty chemicals are produced by things like people's homes and cars, and by planes and factories. This is called pollution. Pollution also comes from pesticides – chemicals which farmers use to kill insects and other living things that eat crops. These chemicals go into the land, rivers, oceans, and air.

A farmer using pesticides in Germany

Pollution is bad for the health of people, animals, and plants. Air pollution, for example, kills about seven million people every year – and in 2016, the World Health Organization (WHO), which is part of the United Nations, said that 92% of the world's population was living in places with air that was dangerously polluted.

Air pollution

Rubbish

Factories and people already produce 1,300 billion kilograms of rubbish every year. And we are producing more and more all the time because people are buying and using more things. In many countries, shops now sell most things in packaging, and when people buy these things, they throw the packaging away. Most of our rubbish goes in landfills – places where rubbish is put in the ground. Chemicals from the rubbish can then go into the ground and into rivers, and landfills also produce a lot of the greenhouse gas, methane.

A landfill

A lot of rubbish today is made of plastic, which stays in the environment for a long time – possibly even one thousand years – before it decomposes (breaks into smaller and smaller pieces and goes back into the land).

The world's oceans are full of pieces of plastic from things like bags and bottles, and a lot of seabirds and other ocean animals now have these pieces in their bodies. Many of them are dying because of this.

A penguin with some plastic

Fast fashion

People used to keep clothes for a long time, but now clothes can be very cheap to buy, and people who want to be fashionable change what they wear all the time. This is called 'fast fashion', and it is a big problem for the environment. Making clothes produces a lot of pollution – and when

Fast fashion in Italy

people buy more clothes, they throw away more, so there is more waste, too. In the USA, many people throw away more than 30 kilograms of clothes every year.

Disappearing species

There are millions of different animals, plants, and other living things on Earth. It took about four billion years for all these species to develop, but today, many of them are in danger, because of climate change and pollution, and because we are destroying their habitats – the places where they live and get food. In the next one hundred years, some people think that between 30% and 50% of all the animal and plant species on Earth will become extinct – none of these species will be alive any more.

The world's rainforests are home to about half of all the living things on Earth, but every year, the world loses about 90,000 square kilometres of rainforest. Companies are cutting down and selling the trees, and using the land to build roads, houses, and farms. The rainforests are also disappearing because climate change is producing hot, dry summers in some places, so more forest fires are happening by accident.

The world's waters are changing, too. People catch billions of fish and sea animals every year, so the populations of many species are getting smaller. Fishing, the rise in sea temperatures, and pollution are also destroying coral reefs – the only home of many sea animals and plants.

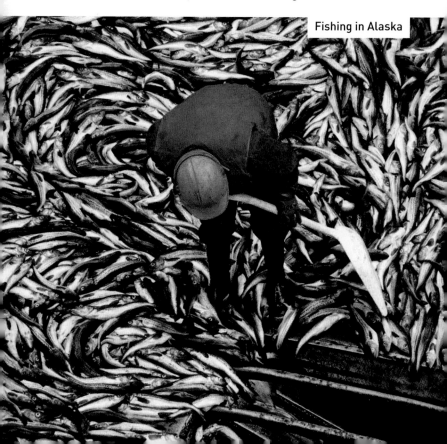

Fishing in Alaska

Many of Earth's animals are in danger from hunting. In the 1990s, there were more than 100,000 tigers around the world, but now, scientists think that there are only between 3,000 and 3,600 living in the wild. Like other animals, they are killed to make things like medicine or clothes.

A tiger

Modern farming puts many species in danger, too, because of the chemicals that are used. Farm pesticides kill the insects that eat crops, but they are also killing the insects that many plants need in order to grow and produce fruit or seeds. This is a big problem for farmers who are trying to produce things like oranges, tomatoes, chocolate, and coffee.

Pesticides are not the only issue with modern farming. In traditional farming – the old way of farming – farmers kept some seeds from their plants in order to grow crops the next year. The seeds all looked the same, but there were actually lots of different species. That was good for farming, because some species grow better in different weather. But since 1950, many farmers have begun to buy their seeds, and when they do this, they often get only a few plant species. So when the weather is not right, or if the climate changes, the farmers may not get good crops. Also, because of this, a lot of different species of food plants have disappeared, or are in danger of disappearing.

5   Protecting Earth

In the 1970s and 1980s, groups of governments and scientists around the world began to meet to talk about the problems of the world's environment. Many people are trying to find answers to these problems, and we are only slowly beginning to make changes to the way we live.

Sustainable energy

Most of the world's energy today comes from burning fossil fuels – fuel from under the ground which is made from animals or plants that lived many thousands of years ago. When we burn fossil fuels, they produce a lot of greenhouse gases, which some scientists think are causing climate change. But fossil fuels can produce energy cheaply, and for this reason, many people have not wanted to stop using them.

In December 2015, countries from around the world met in Paris to talk about climate change. They said that they would slowly stop using fossil fuels, so now many people are working hard to develop sustainable energy. This is energy which produces little or no pollution; and it is made in ways that we can use again and again, or from things that we will always have.

Most sustainable energy today comes from wind, water, or the sun. We get wind energy from wind turbines – big machines that make electricity when the wind turns them.

Other machines can use the energy from moving water in rivers or the sea to make electricity. We can also use solar energy from the sun.

Wind turbines   Collecting energy from moving water

There are many other ways to produce sustainable energy. Some new cars burn a gas called hydrogen to make energy. And in some places, people are making electricity from geothermal energy – heat from under the ground. Iceland already gets most of its energy in this way, and Kenya also uses geothermal energy.

But there are some problems with sustainable energy, too. It cannot easily produce as much electricity as fossil fuels – and we can only get energy from wind and the sun when the weather is right. Also, making the equipment that produces sustainable energy can cause problems for the environment.

Collecting solar energy   Collecting geothermal energy

Cutting waste

In many countries around the world, rubbish is recycled – used again to make something new. In these countries, when people throw away their rubbish, they put things like plastic, glass, and paper in different rubbish boxes, and these are then collected and recycled. Old glass, for example, is taken away and melted, and then made into new bottles or other things.

In Germany and Austria, more than 60% of rubbish is recycled. Curitiba in Brazil is also cutting waste. In this city, two-thirds of all rubbish is recycled. This keeps the city clean, and it produces jobs for local people, too.

In Cairo, Egypt, there are no special organizations for recycling, but 70,000 people called the Zabbaleen go from house to house collecting rubbish. They then take it back to their homes and decide what to do with everything. Most of the things that they collect are used or sold again.

Recycling boxes

The Zabbaleen in Egypt

There is another answer to the problem of rubbish: using and buying fewer things. New online companies are helping people to borrow things when they need them, instead of buying them. Some of these companies try to help people who need things like sports or cooking equipment. They bring these people together with others in the same town or city who have these things and who are happy to lend them.

Many people are beginning to make products in a more sustainable way, too. In Finland, for example, one organization is working with companies to produce clothes which are made from recycled waste, and which will look new for many years – so people will not need to throw them away. To produce less pollution, many other companies are also making things from recycled or natural materials, and trying to use less packaging.

Conservation

Because there is a danger that so many plant and animal species may become extinct, many people now work in conservation – trying to save animals and their habitats. Sometimes, conservationists make special places where no roads, factories, or houses are built, and where natural habitats are protected. They also try to stop people hunting wild animals.

Ten years ago in Spain, a species of wild cat called the Iberian lynx was in danger – there were fewer than one hundred alive. Conservation workers helped the lynxes, and stopped people from hunting them – so now they are able to live safely, and can get their favourite food easily. There are about four hundred Iberian lynxes in the wild now.

An Iberian lynx

Some countries have made new laws about fishing and hunting to help other animals that are in danger of extinction. Many people now use special fishing equipment that will not catch ocean animals or seabirds – and in some places, there are laws about how many fish people can catch. Some governments have also tried to stop people moving animals from country to country, and have made it more difficult for hunters to sell animal skins or body parts.

Svalbard seed store

Seeds at Svalbard

Some conservationists work to save plants, too. On one of the cold Arctic islands of Svalbard, one conservationist has done some important work to protect different species of crops. There, in an unusual building 120 metres under a mountain, he has collected millions of different plant seeds from all around the world – for example, seeds for different species of potato, wild rice, and tomatoes. So this may stop these plants from becoming extinct.

Sustainable farming

Many farmers are now trying to work in a sustainable way. In sustainable farming, people are careful about how they use water and energy, and they do not use chemicals which are bad for the environment. They also keep wild places near their fields to protect wild animals and plants; and they do not destroy forests to make new farmland.

Some people farm trees in sustainable forests now, too. In a sustainable forest, people only take some of the trees at one time, and they plant new trees where the old ones were.

6 Health

Because of modern medicine, millions of people now live longer, healthier lives, and we are developing new ways to fight diseases all the time. But in a changing world, there are changing health problems.

Vaccines

Vaccines were one of the first kinds of modern medicine. They are made from living things that are like diseases – so when they are put into our bodies, our bodies learn how to fight a disease before we get it. The first modern vaccine was made in 1796 for a terrible disease called smallpox. Over the next two hundred years, millions of people were given the vaccine, and this finally ended the disease – today, nobody gets smallpox.

In the last 130 years, scientists have made vaccines for polio and many other dangerous diseases. But a lot of people in developing countries – and one in five children in Africa – cannot get the vaccines, or do not know about them. So people still die from diseases that we can easily prevent.

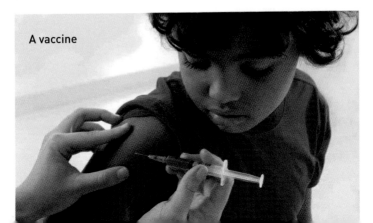

A vaccine

Malaria

One of the most dangerous diseases today is called malaria, and it kills half a million people a year. People die from malaria in parts of Asia, South and Central America, the Caribbean, and Europe – but 90% of deaths from malaria are in Africa.

The disease comes from small insects called mosquitoes. In some countries, local governments and organizations use pesticides to kill mosquitoes, and they give people malaria medicines. Many people are also given mosquito nets – special covers for their beds – to stop mosquitoes from biting them at night.

Happily, some countries are now winning the fight against malaria. In Sri Lanka in 1999, 260,000 people became ill with malaria; in 2016, after a lot of work against the disease, nobody got it.

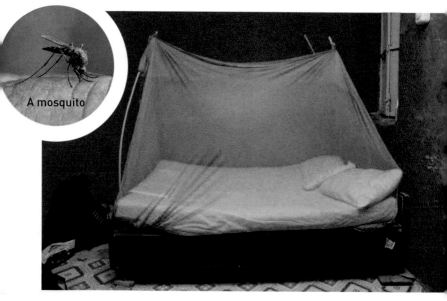

A mosquito

A mosquito net

HIV/AIDS

In the second half of the twentieth century, scientists discovered a new disease called HIV/AIDS, which was killing people around the world. They developed medicines for HIV/AIDS, and a lot of people with the disease now live long, healthy lives. But every year, many people are still dying from the disease and the illnesses which it brings – and in 2015, there were more than one million deaths. 800,000 of these were in countries in Africa, where many people cannot get or pay for medicines – and there were also thousands of deaths from HIV/AIDS in other parts of the world.

Other diseases

New diseases sometimes develop, and these can become a problem very quickly. This happens because diseases can change and become more dangerous. Some diseases can move from animals to people, and they can go from place to place very fast. When someone gets a disease, they may not feel ill for a few days, but in that time, they can give the disease to other people – and get on a plane and fly across the world, taking the disease to other countries.

The World Health Organization watches for dangerous diseases, and WHO doctors travel to places when they are needed. In December 2013, people in Guinea, Liberia, and Sierra Leone, in West Africa, began to get a dangerous disease called Ebola. In the next two years, the disease killed 11,000 people there. But many very brave doctors, and the WHO, stopped Ebola before it could go right across Africa and around the world.

It is difficult to protect people from a terrible disease like Ebola. But while doctors in West Africa were helping people who already had the disease, groups of local people were

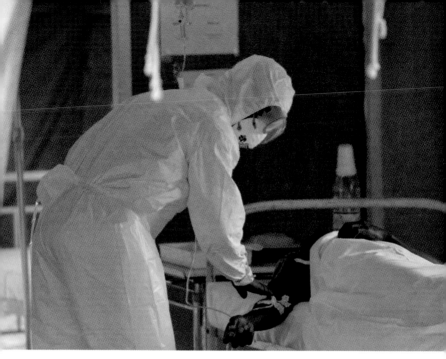

An Ebola doctor in Ivory Coast, West Africa

also visiting towns and villages to try and prevent it. In these places, there were often no toilet or water systems, or the systems were not very good. With help from these groups, people were able to wash carefully, and to stay away from places where they were in danger from the disease. This probably saved a lot of lives.

Antibiotics

In our bodies and all around us, there are many very, very small living things called bacteria. Some of these bacteria are very important for our bodies, but others can cause problems. Antibiotics are medicines which kill bacteria. They have saved millions of lives – but antibiotics also kill some of the healthy bacteria that are good for our bodies. Some of the unhealthy bacteria that antibiotics fought against are now becoming dangerous again, because we have used antibiotics too much. Slowly, some bacteria have become stronger, so antibiotics cannot kill them any more.

Scientists are now trying to develop new antibiotics very quickly, before we lose one of our best ways of fighting diseases. They are also asking doctors, and the people who take these medicines, to use them carefully – they want doctors to choose the right antibiotic for each illness or disease, and they want people to take them at the right time and for long enough, but only when they really need them.

Modern health problems

In the past, most people worked on their feet and moved their bodies all day, so they had lots of exercise. They also mostly ate natural foods like fruit, vegetables, fish, and meat. Today, many people sit in front of a computer all day at work, and often eat a lot of sweet foods, or foods that are made in factories. This can be a big danger to their health.

Sitting at a desk all day can be unhealthy.

The disease that causes most deaths in the world today – three in every ten – is heart disease. But many of these deaths need not happen, and are caused because people have not exercised or eaten well enough. Not exercising, or eating unhealthy food, can sometimes cause another dangerous disease – diabetes. When someone has diabetes, there is too much sugar in their blood. In the last twenty years, there has been a big rise in the number of deaths from diabetes – and almost 10% of the world's population now has this disease.

Smoking is another very big health problem, and it causes more than six million deaths a year. There are lots of very dangerous chemicals in cigarettes, so smokers can get many diseases. Around the world, fewer people smoke today than twenty years ago, but there were still more than 1.1 billion smokers in 2015. This is not just a health problem for cigarette smokers. Nearly half of all the children in the world are taking cigarette smoke into their bodies every day because they have to spend time near people who smoke.

Cigarettes

Many people are also worried about new health problems that are caused by computers and cell phones. When people sit for too long in front of a computer, they can get problems with their eyes, arms, necks, and backs. And when they use computers and cell phones at night, it is often more difficult for them to sleep. Some scientists also think that cell phones may cause health problems because of a kind of energy which they produce called radiation.

Computers and phones may cause health problems.

7   Human rights

In December 1948, the United Nations produced an important declaration called the Universal Declaration of Human Rights. This says that all people everywhere have the same rights – it does not matter where you come from or who you are.

The declaration talks about things like the right to live freely, without danger to your life or health, and the right to have food and medicine, to go to school, and to work.

Women

The Universal Declaration of Human Rights says that there should be gender equality in the world – men and women should have the same rights and chances in life. But although there have been good changes to many women's lives in the last one hundred years, gender equality is still an important global issue.

Around the world, women get less money than men for the work that they do, and this is only changing very, very slowly. Women also do a lot more unpaid work than men – work that they do not get money for, like housework, or caring for children and for friends and family who are ill or old. Women do more housework than men in every country in the world. Women are also the poorest people in the world. Even in the richest country, the USA, the poorest adults are women who are caring for children.

Only a few of the most important leaders in the world are women: in 95% of countries, the president or head of

A woman and child cooking in India

government is a man; and many countries have never had a woman leader. And in almost every kind of work, it is more difficult for women to get the top jobs.

Education

The Universal Declaration of Human Rights says that every child has the right to go to school. But around the world, millions of children do not get an education. Often, this is because families do not have enough money, and the children have to work instead, even when they are very young. Many children also lose their education when schools are closed because there is war in their country.

Some girls have to get married when they are young, and if they have babies, the girls then have to leave school. In some places, too, people try to stop girls reading books and getting a job – because they want them to stay at home.

In the Swat Valley in north-west Pakistan, where Malala Yousafzai lived, a group called the Taliban tried to stop girls getting an education. In 2009, when she was eleven years old, Malala began to write on the internet about how difficult it was for girls to go to school in her town. But the Taliban did not like this, and in October 2012, a man got onto her school bus and shot her. Luckily, she lived, and she continues to fight for every child's right to education today.

Malala Yousafzai

Slavery and work

The Universal Declaration of Human Rights also talks about the right to be free. But about 29 million people in the world are slaves – they must work for others, and they get no pay. Using people in this way is against the law everywhere, but in almost every country, some people still keep slaves. These people use violence against slaves to make them work or do what they want. More than a quarter of all slaves are children.

People who are free and who get money for their work also have important rights. The Universal Declaration of Human Rights says that everyone has the right to work in a place where they are safe and comfortable. It says that there must be equality of pay – people must get the same money for doing the same job – and fair pay – people must get enough money for the work that they do. It also says that workers must have holidays and rest.

But around the world, many workers are underpaid or paid late, or do not get fair pay. Some experience violence, and many have to work in dangerous places. One of these places was the Rana Plaza factory in Bangladesh, which fell down in 2013, killing more than 1,100 people. Most of these people were factory workers who made clothes for high-street shops. But the building was not strong enough for the machines which these people used to do their work.

Rana Plaza factory in Bangladesh

8   **Migration**

Because of globalization, it is becoming easier and easier for people to migrate – to move from one country to another. So in the last fifty years, migration has risen by nearly 100% – and it is growing every year.

Refugees

Many people leave their countries to escape war, or terrible problems like floods. These people are called 'refugees'.

Since World War Two, there have been more than 150 wars, and most of these have been in developing countries. Many of the wars of the twentieth century were between different countries or groups of countries. But a lot of the wars in the twenty-first century have been civil wars – wars between different groups in the same country.

Because of wars and violence in Syria and Afghanistan, and in some African countries, like Somalia, Eritrea, and Sudan, more than 65 million people had to leave their homes in 2015. This is the biggest and most terrible time of world migration since World War Two, when millions of Europeans became refugees to escape from Hitler's Nazis.

Most of the refugees who left their homes in 2015 moved to other countries in Asia or Africa, but many decided to travel to Europe. That year, more than one million people made dangerous journeys from North Africa to Europe by boat – and since then, many more people have crossed the Mediterranean looking for a new life. Refugees sometimes pay a lot of money to people who promise to help them – but

Refugees arriving in Greece

A refugee boat

often, they are put in old boats with too many other people, and the boats break into pieces in the water. Italian and Greek coastguards – officers who keep people safe in and around the sea – save many people when this happens, but they cannot help everybody. In 2016, more than 5,000 people died when they were trying to cross the Mediterranean.

Economic migration

Many people decide to migrate from one country to another because they want to find a new job or a new home, or get better education and healthcare for their families.

In some ways, it can be good for a country when lots of people migrate from it. Often, people who migrate send money home to help their family and friends. Sometimes, they learn new skills while they are away, and then return to their home country and use those skills to help make other people's lives better. When there are fewer people in a country, there is also sometimes more land, work, and money for the people who still live there.

But if a lot of younger people leave a country, this can be a problem, because then there may not be enough people to work. This problem becomes bigger when the people who leave have important skills. And because people leave, fewer children are born in the country, and the population becomes even smaller.

9   Technology

The world's richest countries began to industrialize 250 years ago, and since then, technology has changed the lives of nearly everyone on Earth. We have produced wonderful new machines like telephones, cars, and computers, and modern medicine has saved many lives. People can now travel across the world in hours, not weeks – and scientists have sent machines to Mars! So, can new technology give us the answers to some of today's global issues, or does it bring new problems, too?

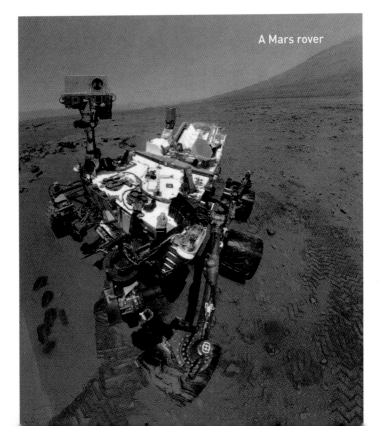

A Mars rover

Communicating by text message and social media

Communication

In 1876, the first telephone was used in the USA by Alexander Graham Bell – and communication changed forever. But today, many people are speaking by telephone less, and are communicating instead by text message, social media, and Skype. Some reports say that, around the world, more than eighteen trillion messages are now sent every day.

People are communicating online more and more in other ways, too. Today, anyone who wants to can write a kind of online diary called a blog. They can write about what matters to them – the books, food, or clothes that they like, or their ideas about different issues, for example. Thousands of people will read what they say. Many people also make vlogs – they use video to give themselves a voice that lots of people will hear.

Vlogging

So it is now quicker, easier, and cheaper to communicate with people for work, or with friends. But many people think that there are problems with these ways of communicating. Many young people never want to turn off their phones, and they use social media late into the night. They go out less, and often make friends with people online who they never meet.

Cyberbullying – when people say unkind things to other people or about other people on social media or in online messages – is a problem that is growing, too. There has always been bullying among young people; but it is easier to be unkind in a message. It is also more difficult for teachers and parents to see cyberbullying and stop it. And for the person who is bullied, there is no escape, because the bullying happens even when they are in their own home.

People put their best photos, and stories about good times they have had, on social media. So, anyone who is finding life hard may easily start to think that other people are happier and better than them, and feel lonely.

Cyberbullying

The internet

Since the 1990s, when people began using the internet, it has become very easy – in most countries – to get information about anything, in almost any place and at any time. The internet has also made it easier to learn, through online lessons and using online study programmes which are open to anyone.

But because we now use the internet for so many things, like shopping, talking to friends, studying, and listening to music, there is a lot of information online about the way we all live. Companies buy this information, and then use it to sell us things. So, when a person in Tokyo buys train tickets online to get to Hiroshima in the west of Japan, she may get messages on her computer about restaurants and hotels in Hiroshima from companies who want her to eat or stay there. Many people do not like it when companies buy and sell information about them in this way, because they think that everyone should have the right to keep information about themselves secret.

Criminals get information about us from the internet, too. They can use the internet to steal money from people, or to take people's names and information about them and pretend to be them. Many companies are now working to try and keep people safer online – and the police talk to schools and many different organizations about how to use the internet carefully.

While people in rich countries can get online almost everywhere, many of the world's poorest people have never been able to use the internet. A 2015 report by the United Nations said that billions of people who live in developing countries still cannot use the internet in their homes and villages. But many organizations are now trying to bring the internet to parts of the world that are not yet online. One of these organizations has developed special computers that do not use a lot of electricity, and another sends people who know all about computers to developing countries to start up internet systems there.

Artificial intelligence

Scientists can now build computers that do jobs which in the past, only people could do. This is called 'artificial intelligence'. People are already using artificial intelligence more and more – for example, when they play video games, listen to music apps like Spotify or Sony Music Unlimited, or use 'satellite navigation' (a computer system in a car that helps the driver to find their way on a journey).

Many people think that artificial intelligence will make our lives safer and easier. 'Driverless cars' are coming to our roads, and there are now more and more machines that can do jobs around the home, like cleaning and washing-up. Machines will do many of the boring jobs that we used to do by hand, some say, and they will also do dangerous work like fighting fires. But some people worry about artificial intelligence. Will it leave any jobs for us, they ask? And the famous scientist Stephen Hawking talked about another problem of artificial intelligence in 2014. Perhaps, he said, machines will one day start to control us.

Other new technologies

One important new technology is 'nanotechnology' – a new technology that uses things which are very, very small (called 'nanoparticles') to do important jobs. Scientists have already used nanotechnology to make sports equipment, because nanoparticles are not heavy, but are very, very

A machine that can do jobs around the home

A driverless car

strong. They are also used in some clothes and healthcare products. Scientists are now looking at how we can use nanotechnology to make safe drinking water for people. In the future, nanotechnology may also help us to take pollution out of our rivers and seas.

Scientists can now copy DNA to make new living things. This technology is called 'cloning', and it helps scientists to develop new medicines and foods. Scientists usually copy just a few plant or animal cells, but they have also copied real animals like sheep, horses, and dogs. Will they make copies of people one day? Many people worry about this, and think that it would be dangerous and wrong.

There are other new technologies that use DNA. Learning about DNA has helped the police to find many criminals, because each person's DNA is different. It can also tell doctors a lot about our future: we can now pay for something called 'genome sequencing', a study of our DNA. When doctors look at this study, they can see the different diseases that we may get in our lives.

'Cloned' or copied dogs

10   Thinking locally

People around the world are working together to try and find global answers to global issues. Here are some examples of great things that they are doing.

Sustainable fashion, Hong Kong

In 2007, in Hong Kong, Christina Dean started an organization called Redress, because she wanted fashion companies to produce less waste.

When Dean visited a landfill in Hong Kong in 2013, she saw lots of old clothes there, and she decided to show people how to recycle them. Each month for the next year, she visited a clothes recycling centre and chose about thirty new outfits (a dress, or a top with a skirt or trousers). So, after a year, she had worn 365 different recycled outfits. When people heard about what she was doing, they started to think and talk more about the problems of fast fashion.

Christina Dean

'Chefugees', Madrid

In Madrid, Spain, a group called Madrid for Refugees have found a great new way to help refugees in the city. Every month, they have special 'Chefugee' dinners, where the food is cooked by a refugee who is looking for work as a chef – a cook – in Madrid. People pay to come to the dinners, and the group use this money to help refugees who are living in the city. The Chefugee dinners also help the people who cook them because the dinners are a good way for them to find work in restaurants or cafés in Madrid.

City farms, Havana

Before 1989, a lot of Cuba's food and fuel was imported – it was bought from other countries. But in the early 1990s, it became difficult for Cuba to import things, so people there could not get what they needed, and many did not have enough to eat. Because of this, in Havana, people began to grow their own food inside the city – in small, empty places between the buildings, and even on the roofs of houses. There are small city farms all over Havana now, and more than 350 square kilometres of land in the city is used for farming.

Thinking locally like this, the people of Havana have made the environment of their city better, and they can also now produce all the food that they need themselves.

A city farm in Havana

A village school, West Bengal

When Babar Ali was a nine-year-old boy, he used to walk ten kilometres a day from his village to his school in Beldanga, in West Bengal, India. Ali's parents were not rich, but his father had enough money to send him to school. On the way to school, Ali saw many children working in the fields. They could not go to school because their families did not have enough money, and they had to work. So Ali decided to help them. After he came home from school every day, he began to give lessons to the children in his village: he explained the things that he was studying at school to them.

Ali started with a class of eight children from his village, and lessons were under a tree outside his parents' house. More and more boys and girls came to Ali's lessons, and the class under the tree grew into a school. Teachers and organizations began to help him, and give him money. Today, Ali's school teaches over eight hundred students. Some of his first students have become teachers, too!

Babar Ali

Cleaning the oceans, Pacific

When Boyan Slat, from the Netherlands, was sixteen years old, he went to Greece – and in the sea there, he saw lots of pieces of plastic. Slat knew that the plastic was very dangerous for all the animals in the ocean, so he wanted to do something about it.

At school, Slat had an idea. There were five places in the ocean which had a lot of plastic, so Slat made plans for a barrier – a kind of wall – near the bottom of the sea in those places, to collect the plastic. He knew that fish and other sea animals would be able to swim under the barrier, and he wanted to recycle all the plastic.

Slat began studying at university, but then he decided to leave to build the first barrier. He had no money, and no one was interested in his ideas at first. But then he talked about the barrier in an online video, and people began to give him money. Slat now hopes that he will be able to build his first barrier in the Pacific. He says that five years after the barrier is built, there will be 50% less plastic there.

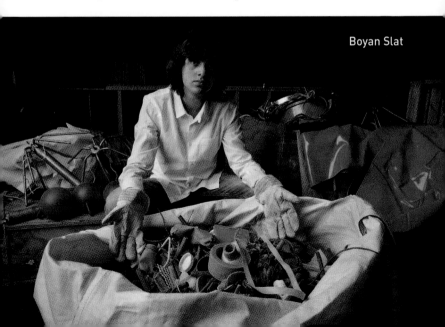

Boyan Slat

Fairtrade

Organizations can make a big difference, too. A lot of the world's best coffee comes from Ethiopia, Colombia, and Guatemala, but often, the big companies that buy the coffee do not give farmers much money for growing it – so while the companies

get richer, the farmers get poorer. Some producers now work with an organization called Fairtrade. Fairtrade helps farmers to get better prices for their products, and to make their farms places where workers' rights are protected, and food is produced without damaging the environment. When you buy products with something called the FAIRTRADE Mark, you know that they come from small farms or organizations that are working towards these goals.

Fairtrade started in 1988, when the first Fairtrade coffee from Mexico was sold into supermarkets in the Netherlands. In the late 1980s and early 1990s, Fairtrade organizations developed in other European and North American countries – and in 1997, they were all brought together in one big organization, which is now called Fairtrade International. Today, more than 1.65 million producers in 74 countries work with Fairtrade, and they produce everything from crops like bananas and tea, to chocolate and cotton clothes.

Fairtrade bananas

One organization which works with Fairtrade is BANAFRUCOOP in Colombia. BANAFRUCOOP was started in 2007 by a group of 26 producers, who were all growing bananas in small fields. Fairtrade asks the organizations that work with it not to use a lot of pesticides, so BANAFRUCOOP had to find more people to work in their fields. That made new jobs for local people, so now each producer has about eleven workers.

Fairtrade also helped BANAFRUCOOP to introduce modern and sustainable ways of farming. So the organization, which produced only 4,800 tonnes of bananas in 2009, produced 6,020 tonnes in 2012. BANAFRUCOOP is always paid the Fairtrade Minimum Price or more for a box of bananas, so the producers know that they will always get $9.80 or more for every box.

* * *

Ideas like these can only help some people, or fix a small part of one of today's many global issues. But in the last fifty years, there have been several important studies which have looked carefully at global issues – and all these studies have agreed that there are no easy answers to these great problems. There are only thousands of small answers – and it is these small answers which will help to take us forward to a better future.

In one hundred years, perhaps people like us will be able to travel easily into space. What will they see when they look back at Earth? Will they see dirty rivers, forests that are smaller than ever before, and an Arctic that has no ice? Perhaps they will see a world that is keeping its environment and its future safe – a fairer world where nobody goes to bed hungry, and people live healthier, happier lives.

astronaut *(n)* a person who works and travels in space

cause *(v & n)* to be the reason why something happens

chemical *(n)* something that is found in things like pesticides and cleaning products, and which causes problems like pollution

collect *(v)* to take things from different people or places and bring them together

communicate *(v)* to give information or ideas to another person; **communication** *(n)*

coral reef *(n)* a big, hard line of rock in the sea that is made of coral (a type of sea animal that looks like a plant)

crop *(n)* a plant that is grown for food, usually in large numbers and on a farm

declaration *(n)* an important message or notice about something, usually given by an important person or group

develop *(v)* to grow slowly, become bigger, or change into something different or better; to build or make

DNA *(n)* the chemical in an animal or a plant that contains information about how it looks or what it is like

Earth *(n)* this world

economy *(n)* how a country spends its money and makes, buys, and sells things; **economic** *(adj)*

education *(n)* the teaching and learning in a school or university

electricity *(n)* a type of energy that we use for heat and light, and to make machines work

energy *(n)* Energy comes from the sun, electricity, gas, etc., and it is used to make machines work and to make heat and light.

environment *(n)* the air, water, land, animals, and plants around us

equipment *(n)* special things that you need for doing something

exercise *(n & v)* moving your body to keep it strong and well

flood *(n & v)* When there is a flood, a lot of water covers the land.

fuel *(n)* anything that you burn to make heat

gas *(n)* something that you can smell but not touch, like air

global *(adj)* coming from, or being about or between, two or more countries

government *(n)* the group of people who control a country

human rights *(n)* what people can have and do, for example the right to speak freely

hunt *(v)* to chase animals to kill them

insect *(n)* a very small animal that has six legs

issue *(n)* an important problem

law *(n)* A law says what people can or cannot do in a country.

leader *(n)* a person who tells a group of people or a country what to do

local *(adj)* in or from the place that is near you

material *(n)* something flat and soft that you use to make clothes; what you use to make into something, often a product

melt *(v)* when something changes, or is made to change, from hard to soft because of heat

migration *(n)* when large numbers of people move from one place to another

ocean *(n & adj)* a very big sea; of or from the sea

organization *(n)* a group of people who work together for a special reason

package *(n & v)* something that comes by post, with material like paper or a box around it to protect it; **packaging** *(n)*

plastic *(n)* a material that is made by people, and used for making many different things, for example water bottles

polluted *(adj)* when water, air, or the land contains dirty and dangerous chemicals, gases, etc.; **pollution** *(n)*

population *(n)* the number of people who live in a place, for example a city, a country, or the world

prevent *(v)* to stop something from happening

produce *(v)* to make or grow something, often for selling

product *(n)* something that people make or grow to sell

protect *(v)* to keep somebody or something safe

rainforest *(n)* a forest in a hot part of the world where there is a lot of rain

rise *(v & n)* to go up or get higher

scientist *(n)* a person who studies science (natural things)

seed *(n)* the small, hard part of a plant from which a new plant grows

skill *(n)* a thing that you can do well, usually because you have done it again and again

social media *(n)* types of communication that allow people to send messages and information online, for example Facebook and Twitter

space *(n)* the place above the sky and beyond Earth, where the sun and stars are

species *(n)* a group of animals or plants that are the same and can make new animals or plants together

sustainable *(adj)* using natural products and energy, or growing things in a way that does not damage the environment

system *(n)* a group of things, parts, or equipment that work together

technology *(n)* knowing about science (natural things) and about how things work, and using this to build and make new things

temperature *(n)* how hot or cold a thing or a place is

throw away *(v)* to get rid of rubbish or something that you do not want

violence *(n)* when someone tries to hurt or kill another person

war *(n)* fighting between countries or between groups of people

waste *(n & v)* things that people throw away because they are not useful; not using something valuable in a useful way

wealth *(n)* a lot of money, land, or houses, for example that a person, country, or organization has

The world as 100 people

How unfair is our world? To understand this, let us say that the world population in 2016 was not about 7.5 billion, but that it was 100 people. How many of these 100 people had an easy, comfortable life?

Of these 100 people, …

22 people had no place to stay. Some of them moved from place to place. Others lived on the streets of a big city.

12 people went to bed hungry at night, but many other people threw away good food.

10 people could not find clean, safe drinking water. **13** more people had to walk a long way to get it.

11 people did not know how to read or write.

33 people had very few rights, and more of these people were women than men.

50 people were poor and lived on very little money.

Global issues

Climate change
Pollution is changing the world's climate. Storms are becoming worse, and global temperatures and sea waters are rising.

Food
The world produces enough food for everyone, but the poorest people often cannot get it – and a lot of food is also wasted. About 800 million people are hungry every day.

Growing population
In 1950, the world's population was 2.6 billion people. By 2050, that number will be about 9.5 billion!

Habitat loss
People and climate change are destroying habitats like rainforests and coral reefs. Because of this, many animal and plant species are disappearing.

Health
Many people die from diseases that are preventable. This is because they cannot get clean water, food, or medicines. Our modern way of life can also be bad for our health.

Human rights
All people should have the same rights. But many people still do not have the same rights in education or work, and there are still many problems with gender equality.

Inequality

Some people and some countries have a lot of money. In other places, people are very poor. The richest few percent of the population have most of the world's wealth.

Migration

Millions of people have to leave their homes every year because of war, violence, economic problems, or climate change.

Pollution

Factories, farms, and cars use and produce dangerous chemicals. These chemicals cause air and water pollution.

Technology

Technology has helped to build our modern world. But new technologies also bring new problems and dangers.

War

Every year, thousands of people die fighting, or have to leave their homes.

Water

Millions of people die because they cannot get enough clean water to drink and use at home.

Global Issues

ACTIVITIES

Think ahead

1 **What do you think you are going to read about in this book?
Tick (✓) the things.**

animals ☐	farming ☐	money ☐
big cities ☐	holidays ☐	football ☐
crime ☐	books ☐	the internet ☐
rubbish ☐	diseases ☐	the weather ☐

2 **Do you agree with these statements? Write Yes or No.**

1 The world is a fair place. _____

2 We should all recycle most of our rubbish. _____

3 Technology will fix the world's environmental problems.

_____

4 One day, the world's population will stop growing.

_____

5 Computers and other new technologies will become
dangerous one day. _____

3 **RESEARCH Before you read, find out the answers to
these questions.**

1 What was the population of your country fifty years ago?

2 What is the population of your country now?

3 Find the names of three species of animal that are in danger
in your country.

Chapter check

CHAPTER 1 Complete the sentences with words from the text.

1 Astronauts can see how beautiful Earth is, but also how it is _____.
2 The world's great _____ are becoming smaller.
3 There is more _____ in the ocean every year.
4 Many people around the world go to bed _____.
5 Many children cannot go to _____.

DISCUSS What do you think is the most important global issue today? Why is it so important?

CHAPTER 2 Complete the sentences with the correct numbers.

3.6   7.5   9.5   30   65   100

1 In 2016, about _____ billion people lived on Earth.
2 By 2050, the world population will be about _____ billion.
3 More than 25% of Japan's population is over _____.
4 _____% of the people on Earth lived in cities in 1950.
5 Some megacities of the future will have as many as _____ million people in them.
6 In 2017, the world's eight richest people had the same as the poorest _____ billion.

DISCUSS Is the population of your country growing or falling? What is the biggest city in your country?

CHAPTER 3 Are the sentences true, false, or not in the text?

1 There is enough food for the world's population, but many people are hungry.
2 Most food waste happens because of bad farming.
3 It is often cheaper to buy food products from other countries.
4 Eating insects is bad for the environment.
5 Most scientists think that GM crops are safe to eat.

DISCUSS What food that you eat comes from outside your country? What places does it come from?

CHAPTER 4 Correct the underlined words in the sentences.

1 The world's oceans are <u>melting</u> every year.
2 <u>Medicines</u> are used to kill the insects that eat farmers' crops.
3 About seven million people die every year because of air <u>temperatures</u>.
4 Today, the oceans are full of pieces of <u>wood</u>.
5 About <u>a quarter</u> of all Earth's plants and animals live in the world's rainforests.
6 Traditionally, farmers kept <u>trees</u> to use for the next year. Now, most farmers buy them from companies.

DISCUSS How much rubbish do you throw away every week? How can you throw away less rubbish?

CHAPTER 5 Choose the correct answers.

1 People continue to use fossil fuels because they are…
   a   cleaner than other fuels.
   b   cheaper than other fuels.
2 We can get geothermal energy from…
   a   hot places under the ground.
   b   the moving water in rivers.
3 What do the Zabbaleen do in Cairo?
   a   They collect waste for recycling.
   b   They clean the streets.
4 In a sustainable forest, …
   a   all the trees are protected and you cannot use them.
   b   people plant new trees when they take old trees.

DISCUSS How is most energy produced in your country?

CHAPTER 6 Complete the sentences with words from
the text.

1 _____ help our bodies to learn how to fight diseases.
2 _____ is a disease which comes from mosquitoes.
3 Many people with HIV/AIDS now live long lives, but others
   die because they cannot get the right type of _____.
4 Some old diseases are returning because we have used
   _____ too much.
5 Another big health problem in the world is _____,
   which kills six million people every year.

DISCUSS What is the biggest health problem in your country?

CHAPTER 7 Complete the sentences with the words below. There are two extra words which you do not need.

dangerous   Declaration   education
violence   wealthy   work

1 The Universal _____ of Human Rights talks about many things, like women's rights, the right to go to school, and the right to be free.
2 Millions of children have to _____ because their families are poor and need the money.
3 In some places, it is more difficult for girls to get an _____.
4 Some people work in very bad or _____ places.

DISCUSS The Universal Declaration of Human Rights talks about lots of rights, like gender equality, the right to education, and the right to be free. Which of these do you think is most important?

CHAPTER 8 Tick (✓) the two sentences which are true.

1 A lot of wars in the twenty-first century are wars between big groups of countries. ☐
2 In 2015, most refugees travelled to other countries in Asia and Africa. ☐
3 Over 5,000 refugees died in the Pacific in 2016. ☐
4 Economic migration is sometimes bad for the countries people have migrated from. ☐

DISCUSS Do more people migrate to or from your country? Where do they come from/go to?

CHAPTER 9 Match the sentence halves.

1 Communication is quicker and easier now, but…
2 Cyberbullying is very difficult…
3 Online information about people is used by companies, but…
4 Artificial intelligence may make our lives easier, but…
5 Scientists who use cloning usually…

a should those organizations have the right to take it and use it?
b it can be difficult for young people to turn off their phones.
c copy some cells, but they have also copied animals.
d will machines start to control us one day?
e for people to see, stop, or escape.

DISCUSS In 2070, do you think there will be any jobs for people, or will artificial intelligence do everything for us?

CHAPTER 10 Complete each sentence with one word from the text.

1 This group helps people who can cook to find _____ in restaurants or cafés.
2 In the early 1990s, it was difficult for Cuba to _____ food and other things.
3 When Babar Ali was young, he saw that many children could not go to _____.
4 When you buy Fairtrade products, you know that the farmers who produce them are getting a fair _____.

DISCUSS Do you know people or organizations in your city or country that are doing things locally to try to make the world a better place?

Focus on vocabulary

1 Read the clues and complete the word puzzle. What is the mystery word?

1 a person who has to leave their home because of war or terrible things that happen in their country *(n)*
2 a place where we put our rubbish in the ground *(n)*
3 how many people live in a place *(n)*
4 a place where animals live and get food *(n)*
5 when people or countries have a lot more wealth than others *(n)*
6 to change from ice into water *(v)*

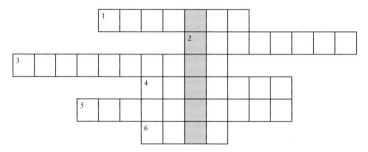

2 Complete the sentences with the words below.

artificial   megacity   slavery   waste

1 A _____ is a place which is home to more than ten million people.
2 Food _____ is a big problem – we throw away a lot of the food that we produce.
3 _____ is when people must work for no money.
4 _____ intelligence, or 'thinking machines', may one day be dangerous for people.

Focus on language

1 Complete the sentences with the relative pronouns *who,* *which, when,* or *where.*

1 The oceans are full of pieces of plastic _____ are dangerous for sea animals.

2 Because of globalization, it is easy to do business with people _____ live thousands of miles away.

3 Some GM crops can grow well in droughts – times _____ there is no rain.

4 Animals are becoming extinct because we are destroying the places _____ they live.

5 There are many people _____ die of diseases because they cannot pay for medicines.

2 **DECODE** Read the two short extracts from the text and answer the questions.

A In 1950, the world had a population of 2.6 billion people, but today, there are more people than ¹that just in China and India. By 2016, there were 7.5 billion people in the world – and ²that number was growing by about one million every five days!

B The population of the Cook Islands, in the Pacific, is falling every year. ³This is because people are having fewer children than before, and because ⁴many are leaving the islands to go to bigger places like New Zealand.

In the two extracts, what do these words refer to?

1 that   2 that number   3 this   4 many

Discussion

1 **COLLABORATE** Read the dialogue. Do you agree with
speaker A or speaker B?

A: I think that GM foods are a good thing.

B: Really? I don't agree. GM crops are very dangerous.

A: Why do you think that?

B: Because we don't know what problems they'll cause in
the future.

A: Can you explain what you mean?

B: Well, for example, they may be bad for our health, or for
the environment. It will take years to find out if GM crops
are safe or not.

A: Hmm. That's a good point.

2 Complete the phrases from exercise 1.

1 I _____ that...

2 Really? I _____.

3 Why _____?

4 Can _____?

5 That's _____.

3 **COMMUNICATE** Discuss the statements below with a partner.
Use the phrases from exercise 2.

1 There will always be wars because people are
naturally violent.

2 Rich people should give most of their money to the poor.

3 Globalization is a bad thing.

1 Read the notes for a presentation about the rainforests and put the headings in the correct place. There is one extra heading which you do not need.

What are the future dangers?   *What can people do?*
What is happening?   *What is the reason for this?*
Why does it matter?

Rainforests in danger

1 _____
   • Millions of trees are cut down or burned every year.
   • Habitats and animal and plant species are disappearing.

2 _____
   • Trees are cut down for paper or wood.
   • Rainforests are destroyed to make farmland / grow crops for rich countries.

3 _____
   • Rainforests are home to half of all animal and plant species on Earth. Many will disappear.
   • Local people get food and medicine from the rainforest.

4 _____
   • Conservationists – make protected places.
   • Farmers – use sustainable farming.
   • People – buy wood and paper from sustainable forests.

2 **Where in the presentation do these points go? Write 1–4.**

a Trees take greenhouse gases out of the air. Cutting them down makes climate change worse. _____

b Companies destroy rainforest areas to get things like gold and fossil fuels from under the ground. _____

c Every year, 90,000 square kilometres of rainforest are destroyed. _____

d People cut down trees to build new towns and roads.

_____

e Government – make new laws to stop people hunting.

3 **Prepare a presentation about one of the global issues below. Think of four headings for your presentation.**

climate change   migration   pollution   water and food

4 **Use this book and the internet to plan your presentation. Take notes and include two or three pieces of information for each heading in your plan.**

5 **COLLABORATE In groups, take turns to talk about your presentation plans. Decide as a group which information is most important to have in each final presentation, and why. Then practise your presentations.**

6 **Take turns to give your final presentation to the class.**

If you liked this Bookworm, why not try...

Animal Kingdom

STAGE 3
Rachel Bladon

From the smallest fly to the biggest elephant, and from fish living at the bottom of the ocean to birds that fly several kilometres above land: this is the animal kingdom, the biggest group of living things in the world. Some are very different; others are the same in many ways – but these mammals, birds, fish, reptiles, amphibians, and invertebrates have all managed to live for thousands and thousands of years. How do they find food, grow, keep safe, and have young - and what is the future for them in this fast-changing world?

Space

STAGE 3
Tim Vicary

Is there anyone who has not looked at the dark sky, and the shining points of light above us, and asked themselves questions about what is out there? Where did our planet come from? When did the universe begin? Could we live on another planet?

Begin a journey into space – where spacecraft travel at thousands of kilometres an hour, temperatures are millions of degrees, and a planet may be hard rock or a ball of gas. In space, everything is extraordinary...